WHOHQ
AF386821

To Parker Jade, Molly May, and Rosalie Joy—
superstars-to-be in whatever they pursue!—CH

To my lovely mother, for always being
an example of overcoming—MDP

PENGUIN WORKSHOP
An imprint of Penguin Random House LLC
1745 Broadway, New York, NY 10019
penguinrandomhouse.com

Design by Taylor Abatiell
Text set in Adobe Garamond Pro

The art was created using Procreate and Photoshop.

Library of Congress Cataloging-in-Publication Data is available.

First published in the United States of America by Penguin Workshop, 2026

Manufactured in China
HH

ISBN 9798217144693
10 9 8 7 6 5 4 3 2 1

The authorized representative in the EU for product safety and compliance is Penguin Random House Ireland, Morrison Chambers, 32 Nassau Street, Dublin D02 YH68, Ireland, https://eu-contact.penguin.ie.

WHOHQ

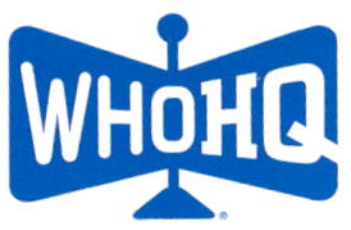

SIMONE BILES

A WHO HQ ILLUSTRATED BIOGRAPHY

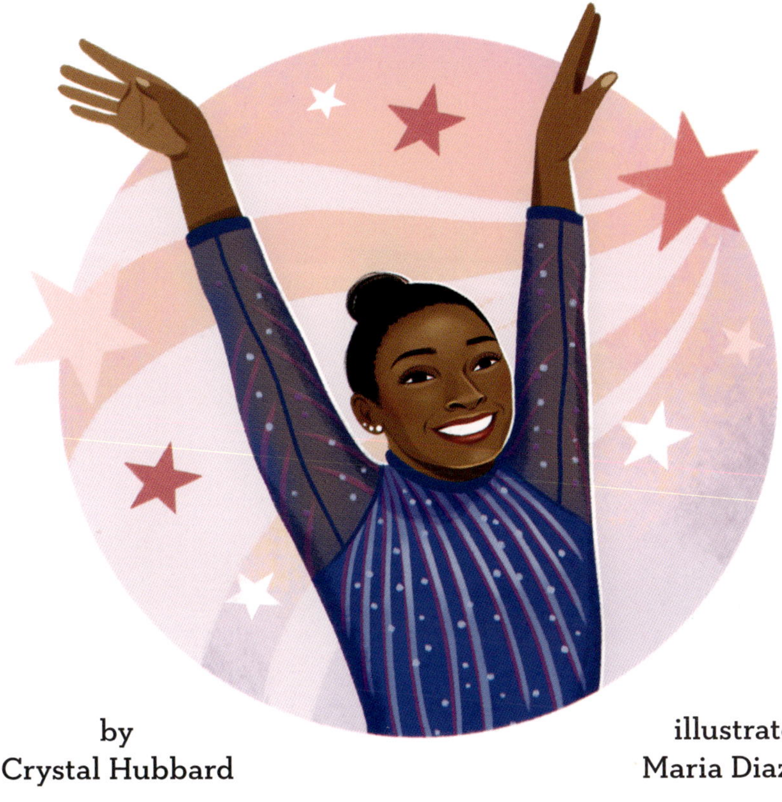

by
Crystal Hubbard

illustrated by
Maria Diaz Perera

PENGUIN WORKSHOP

annon's Gymnastix in Houston, Texas, was a fun place. One day, a six-year-old girl went there on a field trip. Some kids at the gym were not just jumping on trampolines and playing on padded mats. They swung from parallel bars. They gracefully tiptoed along a long beam. They ran across the floor, then bounced into flips, turns, and twirls in the air.

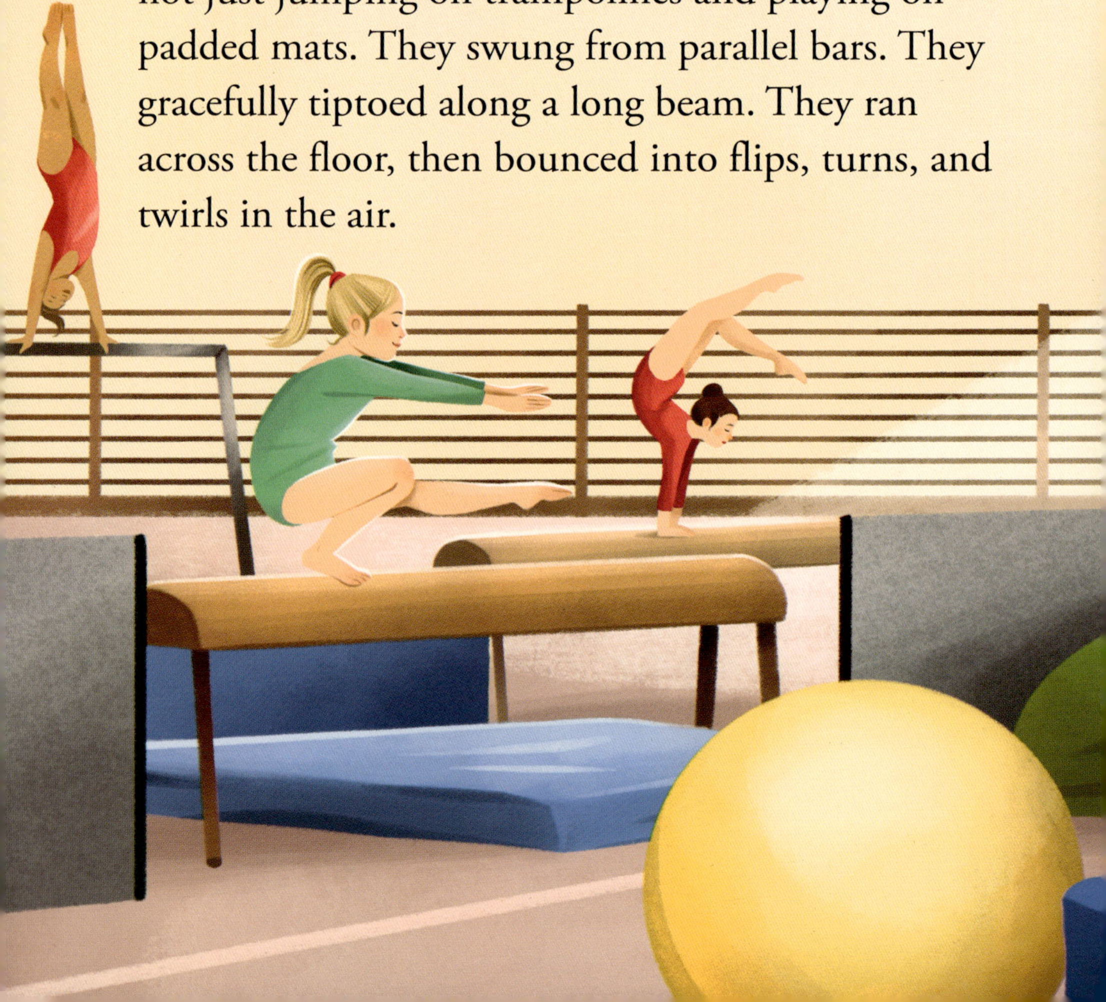

The little girl stepped onto a mat. She did a backflip, copying another gymnast.

A coach saw her and was so impressed, she wanted to contact the little girl's parents so she could train her.

WHO WAS THIS NATURAL ATHLETE?

Simone Arianne Biles was born on March 14, 1997, in Columbus, Ohio. Her early years were difficult. Her mother, Shanon Biles, couldn't care for Simone and her three siblings. Simone's father wasn't involved in the family. The children were in and out of foster care.

Shanon's father, Ron Biles, did not want his grandchildren in foster care. Simone was three years old when Ron and his wife Nellie took in her and her younger sister Adria. Ron's sister Harriet adopted Simone's two older siblings. Ron and Nellie adopted Simone and Adria when Simone was six. "If not for my parents and adoption, I wouldn't be here today," Simone would later say.

Simone called her grandparents Mom and
Dad. She loved her parents and was happy living
with them in Spring, Texas, near Houston. The
gymnastics coach who'd seen Simone at Bannon's
Gymnastix asked Ron and Nellie if she could train
Simone. They eagerly said yes!

Simone was a whirlwind of energy who did flips on furniture and cartwheels across the living room floor. Her parents thought gymnastics would be a good way to spend Simone's extra energy.

Simone learned about every piece of gymnastics equipment and how to use it. Women's gymnastics uses four different pieces of equipment, or apparatuses. For the vault, gymnasts have to run very fast to build momentum. They jump onto a springboard and then push off the vault with their hands. They do flips, tucks, and turns before landing with both feet on a mat.

The balance beam is sixteen feet long but only four inches wide. It's just short of five feet tall. Gymnasts carefully walk, flip, and spin on it.

The uneven bars have a top bar that is just over eight feet high and a lower bar that is about five and a half feet high. The space between the two bars and their height is adjustable to best suit each gymnast's body and style, and the tricks they perform.

The floor exercise takes place on a cushioned mat covering springs. The springs help the gymnasts reach amazing heights when they jump and bounce. The gymnasts have to stay within an area of forty feet by forty feet. If they step into the three-foot border, they lose points.

Simone was seven when she began training with Coach Aimee Boorman. Simone had become very good on each apparatus, but she was especially good at the floor exercise and vault. Being able to run and launch into outstanding strings of flips and turns and strength moves on the mat suited Simone's short, strong body very well. She almost always stuck her landings.

Sticking the landing means finishing without wobbling, fighting to stay balanced, or taking any extra steps. This is important on every apparatus and means not losing points.

Her first national competition was the Women's Junior Olympic National Championships in 2010. She won a gold medal in the floor exercise. She was only thirteen years old!

The next year, Simone moved into a higher level, beginning her elite career. At the American Classic in Huntsville, Texas, she earned first on vault and balance beam. She placed third in the event for best all-around gymnast, or the top combined score from each apparatus.

Simone competed in Huntsville again in the 2012 American Classic. She won first place all-around and on the vault.

When Simone was fourteen years old, she left public school to learn at home. Homeschooling allowed her to spend more time training. She spent around six hours a day in the gym on weekdays, and even more on the weekends. She was a very hard worker. "If they said, 'Do five pull-ups,' I would always want to do ten," Simone said.

Simone became an international senior elite gymnast in 2013. She competed in the City of Jesolo Trophy in Italy. She earned first place in the vault, balance beam, floor exercise, and all-around gymnast. Her effort helped the US team win an overall gold medal.

Simone was built for gymnastics, and she was a very hard worker, but the 2013 Secret US Classic gymnastics meet exposed Simone's weakness. She made mistakes in her routines. She fell badly in her floor exercise and then twisted her ankle at the end of her routine. She couldn't compete in the vault. Her mistakes and injury weighed on her. "I just thought it was the end of the world," Simone said at the time.

Ron and Nellie attended every one of Simone's competitions. As much as they loved Simone, they could see she needed more help than they could give her.

Simone consulted a sports psychologist. That's someone trained in helping athletes deal with the unique troubles they face. Athletes sometimes lose confidence. They sometimes feel panic and anxiety about their performances and skills.

Simone returned to dominate gymnastics competitions. She won best all-around gymnast in the 2013 P&G Gymnastics Championships. That made her the best gymnast in the United States. She also won the all-around gold medal at the 2013 World Championships. That made her the best gymnast in the world! She's the first African American woman to earn that title.

In 2013, she performed a vault routine that was so original, it was named for her. It was called the Biles. In 2015, she won the all-around gold medals in the national and world competitions. Simone won all-around gold medals in every meet she was in during 2014 and 2015.

THE BILES

In elite sports such as figure skating and gymnastics, the first time big, new skills are performed perfectly in competition, they get named for the athlete who originated them. Simone has five skills so difficult, they are named for her: the Biles and Biles II on vault, the Biles on the balance beam, and the Biles and Biles II in the floor exercise.

The Biles II is a vault where Simone does a roundoff into a back handspring onto the vault, and then two back flips in the pike position—an L shape—before landing. It's so difficult because it takes so much strength to reach the height needed to complete two pikes in the air. She's the only female gymnast who has performed this vault in competition!

In 2016, she qualified for her first Olympics, the Summer Games in Rio de Janeiro, Brazil. She won the all-around gold. She left Rio with four gold medals and one bronze. She was the first female American gymnast to do that. She instantly became one of the most famous athletes in the world.

Aimee Boorman, Simone's coach, moved to Florida with her family in 2016. Simone wanted to stay in Texas, close to her family. She signed on with a new pair of coaches, Cecile and Laurent Landi.

Simone won many more tournaments. When the Olympics came back around in Tokyo in 2021, so did Simone's anxiety. The world was watching her. She knew she had to be perfect. That curse of expectation was too heavy.

She performed well but not up to her usual standard. She eventually pulled out of the games. "I felt like it would be a little better to take a back seat, and work on my mindfulness," she explained. "I didn't want the team to risk a medal because of [me]."

A lot of people criticized Simone for leaving the competition. They called her selfish. Simone attended every gymnastics event and cheered for her teammates. Simone stepping back gave other teammates the chance to compete.

Simone competed in the balance beam final and won the bronze medal. She counts that medal as her favorite because it represents her courage to put her mental health ahead of sports achievements. "It's okay sometimes to even sit out the big competitions to focus on yourself, because it shows how strong of a competitor and person that you really are," Simone said.

Simone later told the world that she withdrew from the Tokyo Olympics because of a problem called the twisties. Gymnasts sometimes get confused in the air while twisting and flipping. It's dangerous because the gymnast could land wrong and get hurt badly. Many athletes were proud of Simone for being so open about her mental health.

After a short break, Simone returned to
competition in 2023. Her winning ways continued
right up to the 2024 Olympics in Paris, France.
Simone was twenty-seven years old, and she seemed
stronger than ever in mind and body. She won three
gold medals and one silver. Simone's teammates
earned medals, too. Simone, Sunisa Lee, Jordan
Chiles, Jade Carey, and Hezly Rivera won the team
gold medal. Simone won gold medals in the all-
around individual and vault. She also won silver in
the floor exercise. Sunisa won the bronze for the
individual all-around and uneven bars, and Jade
won bronze in the vault.

CAREER HIGHLIGHTS

Simone has earned eleven Olympic medals, the most ever for an American gymnast. She has won thirty World Championship medals, twenty-three of which are gold. No other gymnast has won so many medals.

Simone has won nine United States national all-around championships. When she won in 2024, she became the oldest gymnast to win the title. She was twenty-seven years old.

President Joe Biden named Simone a Presidential Medal of Freedom recipient in 2022. This is the highest award a civilian can earn in the United States. She was its youngest recipient.

When her 2024 Olympic teammate Jordan Chiles wanted to quit the sport, Simone invited Jordan to train at her gym. Jordan received the coaching and mental health support she needed to turn her career around. She ended up winning a team gold medal in 2024.

Simone has inspired athletes and other people all over the world with her dedication to her sport and her mental health advocacy. She is one of the most accomplished athletes and strongest people the world has ever seen.

BIBLIOGRAPHY

***Books for young readers**

Biles, Simone. *Courage to Soar: A Body in Motion, a Life in Balance*. With Michelle Burford. Grand Rapids, MI: Zondervan, 2016.

*Burk, Rachelle. *The Story of Simone Biles: A Biography Book for New Readers*. Emeryville, CA: Rockridge Press, 2020.

*Daniels, Rachel. *Meet Simone Biles!* Hallandale, FL: Mitchell Lane Publishers, 2024.

*Levit, Joe. *Gymnastics's G.O.A.T.: Nadia Comaneci, Simone Biles, and More*. Minneapolis. Lerner Publications, 2022.

*Loh, Stefanie. *Who Is Simone Biles?* New York: Penguin Workshop, 2023.

*Morgan, Sally. *Trailblazers: Simone Biles: Golden Girl of Gymnastics*. New York: Random House Children's Books, 2020.

*Wetzel, Dan. *Epic Athletes: Simone Biles*. New York: Henry Holt Books for Young Readers, 2020.

WEBSITE

simonebiles.com

TIMELINE

1997	Simone Arianne Biles is born in Columbus, Ohio, on March 14
2000	Placed in foster care with her siblings
2003	Adopted by her mother's father, Ron Biles, and his wife Nellie
	Tries gymnastics for the first time and soon enrolls in formal training
2011	Makes her junior elite gymnastics debut
2013	Wins her first US National Championship and World Championship all-around titles at just sixteen
2015	Becomes the first woman to win three consecutive World all-around titles

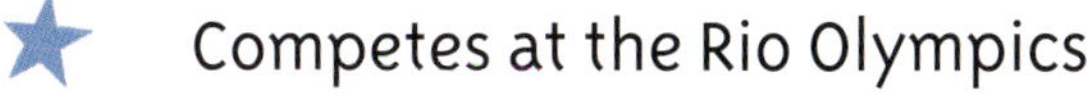

Competes at the Rio Olympics — **2016**

Wins her fourth World all-around title — **2018**

Becomes the first female gymnast to land a triple-double (three twists, two flips) on floor exercise — **2019**

Wins seventh US National Championship — **2021**

Competes at the Tokyo Olympics, withdraws from several events due to the twisties

Returns to competition after a two-year break and becomes the most decorated gymnast of all time — **2023**

Marries NFL player Jonathan Owens on April 22

Competes at the 2024 Paris Olympics — **2024**

Earns the title Sportsperson of the Year from *Sports Illustrated*